IMAGES
of America

FRANCISCAN FRIARS
OF HEBBRONVILLE

IMAGES
of America

FRANCISCAN FRIARS
OF HEBBRONVILLE

Fr. Juan Jose Ibarra, OFM

ARCADIA
PUBLISHING

Published by Arcadia Publishing
Charleston, South Carolina

Printed in the United States of America

Library of Congress Control Number: 2023947931

For all general information, please contact Arcadia Publishing:
Telephone 843-853-2070
Fax 843-853-0044
Email sales@arcadiapublishing.com

Visit us on the Internet at www.arcadiapublishing.com

To the Franciscan friars,
for their presence, sacrifice, and service in Hebbronville

To the community of Hebbronville,
for their welcome, love, and support over the years

CONTENTS

ACKNOWLEDGMENTS

No book is the work of one person. This book would not have been possible without the support and encouragement of a large group of individuals and organizations who enthusiastically contributed their historical photographs and records and offered their support and guidance to this project. My sincere gratitude and deep appreciation to, before anyone else, God for being the source of inspiration and wisdom; the Franciscan Museum of Hebbronville Archives, the Archivo Histórico Franciscano de Zapopan in Mexico, and the Museum Foundation of Hebbronville Archives for their photographic material and their efforts to preserve our history; my fellow Franciscan brothers of the Saints Francis and James Province in Mexico and of the Our Lady of Guadalupe Friary in Hebbronville for giving me the opportunity to serve in this beautiful community; the people of Hebbronville, Texas, and the Our Lady of Guadalupe Parish family in the Diocese of Laredo for their love and support; my family and friends for their help and prayers; and to all who in one way or another made this book possible. Peace and Good!

Unless otherwise noted, all images appear courtesy of the Franciscan Museum of Hebbronville Archives.

INTRODUCTION

The history of the arrival of the Franciscan friars in 1926 to Hebbronville, Texas, escaping the religious persecution in Mexico is an enduring story that resonates today in the hearts and souls of many Franciscans from the Jalisco Province in Mexico and in the people of Hebbronville who, over the years, have worked together with the Franciscans. The friars have been in Hebbronville for almost a hundred years, unlike other communities that welcomed religious orders who eventually returned to their homeland. Soon after their arrival, they built a majestic four-story seminary that is considered a Texas treasure and a preeminent historic architectural landmark in Hebbronville: the Scotus College.

Despite the rich historical narrative and the imposing architectural legacy, many people even some from the immediate area and a majority of youth do not know the captivating story of the Franciscan presence in Hebbronville. There is little historical account of the awareness of the profound sacrifices, trials, and difficulties experienced by these friars, as well as the determination to provide spiritual, educational, and cultural guidance. Visitors and travelers who stop by and take pictures of the towering the Scotus College and its church do not have a clue about the history behind the buildings. Most Texans, not to mention Americans, do not even know where Hebbronville is.

For these reasons, this book presents the history of the Franciscan presence in Texas, the origins of this small community of Hebbronville, and the history of the arrival and the legacy of the Franciscans in Hebbronville and its surrounding communities. A story of religious persecution in Mexico, Franciscan priests and seminarians finding refuge in a small town in south Texas, their constant presence in the community that welcomed them, and the amazing seminary they helped build, has great historic value and is a story worth telling.

Franciscans is the popular name for the priests and religious men who consecrate their lives to live the Gospel according to the way of St. Francis of Assisi, who founded the Franciscan Order in 1209. Though St. Francis and his companions always referred to themselves as brothers, they have commonly come to be called friars to indicate that their brotherhood is a special kind of religious bond. The official name of the Franciscan Order in Latin is Ordo Fratrum Minorum, translated as Order of Friars Minor (OFM). The word "minor" indicates that the Franciscans are not to be considered important, but instead to be thought of as lesser ones as they go about the world. Franciscans were the first Christian missionaries in the western hemisphere since the voyage of the discovery of the Americas in 1492. The kings of Spain sent Franciscan friars alongside colonizers to the lands of what is now Mexico and the United States. In 1712, Franciscan friars arrived in Texas from the west, what is now New Mexico. Later, Franciscans from the Apostolic Colleges of Queretaro and Zacatecas came to Texas and founded most of the missions. The most recognized among them is Fr. Antonio Margil the Jesús, also known as the Apostle of Texas. Further information on the Franciscan imprint in the culture and civilization of Texas will be presented in chapter one.

The Franciscan friars who planted the foundations of Texas in the 16th century were the ancestors of the Franciscan friars who arrived in Hebbronville years later in 1926. They belonged to the Saints Francis and James Province in Mexico. After a tumultuous time of political conflicts in Mexico and the anticlerical measures established by the Mexican government, the Franciscans lost most of their properties and members. They had to restructure by founding three new Provinces. The Saints Francis and James Province, also known as the Jalisco Province, was formed in 1908 as a union between the Franciscan Provinces of Jalisco and Zacatecas and the two Apostolic Colleges of Guadalupe and Zapopan. The story behind these historic events will be found in chapters two and three.

Chapter four centers around Hebbronville, a small town located around 50 miles from the Mexican border. It is the seat of Jim Hogg County in the state of Texas. To many, it might be unknown or just a dot on the map, but to residents and the Franciscans, it is more than home. The reader will get to know Hebbronville, the Vaquero capital, from its humble origins.

August 6, 1926, is a date that should be honored and remembered by the people of Hebbronville and by the Franciscan friars of the Jalisco Province. This is the date when the three first Franciscan friars arrived in Hebbronville. Their names were Fr. Bernardino Madueño, Fr. José Guadalupe Torres, and Fr. Pascual Ruiz. Their mission was to find shelter in South Texas for the persecuted Franciscans being exiled from Mexico. The friars obtained permission from Bishop Emmanuel Ledvina of the Diocese of Corpus Christi to live in Hebbronville and be in charge of the Parish and its missions and granted them perpetually the ownership of the house to live and form the Franciscan seminarians. Chapters five, six, and seven document the history of the Franciscan presence and legacy in Hebbronville and in the surrounding missions. This history is primarily based on two important documents: *Reseña histórica de la fundación de las casas franciscanas de Hebbronville y Sarita, Texas* (*Historical review of the foundation of the Franciscan friaries of Hebbronville and Sarita, Texas*), written in 1927 by Fr. José María Casillas, OFM (the last Franciscan from the Apostolic College in Guadalupe), and *Los Franciscanos en Hebbronville* (*The Franciscans in Hebbronville*) written in 1931 by Fr. Ángel Ochoa, OFM (one of the first seminarians who arrived in 1926).

This is the story about Hebbronville, Texas and the events that a group of Franciscans from Mexico immortalized with their lives full of boundless hope, talents, illusions, experience, wisdom, youth, and humility to learn. Their story is a lesson about love, devotion, surrender, and sacrifice for others. We give thanks to the ancestral Franciscan friars and the people of Hebbronville for their unwavering belief in life and giving. Because of them and their spirit, we live now.

One

Franciscan Missions in Texas

The first missionaries who introduced Christianity to Texas were Franciscan priests and brothers of the Order of Friars Minor, founded by St. Francis of Assisi in 1209. They came to Mexico in the 16th century, and their successors who went north to Texas in the 17th and 18th centuries, carried their rigorous, Observant worldview with them. Their unique religious culture left a deep imprint on Spanish Texas. Franciscans were no simple followers of the Spanish colonization project—they were, in some ways, its intellectual authors and architects.

The first missionary journeys into Texas came from the west, where the Franciscans had begun evangelizing the Indian pueblos around Santa Fe soon after it was made the capital of New Mexico in 1610. Later, most of the Texas missions were directed from two *conventos* or *colegios* (colleges) of Franciscans in Mexico. These two missionary colleges were the Apostolic College of Propaganda Fide of Santa Cruz at Querétaro (founded in 1683) and the Apostolic College of Propaganda Fide of Nuestra Señora de Guadalupe at Zacatecas (founded in 1707). In 1772, the College of Querétaro surrendered all its missions to the College of Zacatecas and left Texas. Five Texas missions—among them, San José y San Miguel de Aguayo Mission, flagship in San Antonio—were founded by Fr. Antonio Margil de Jesús, who was the president and founder of the College of Guadalupe at Zacatecas. He is considered to be "the Apostle of Texas."

The College of Guadalupe at Zacatecas also supplied 17 missionaries for the 19 villas and 15 missions established by José de Escandón in the new civil province of Nuevo Santander (Tamaulipas and South Texas) between 1749 and 1755. In total, 121 Franciscans of the College of Zacatecas served as missionaries in Texas between 1716 and 1834, with 32 dying in Texas. It is no exaggeration to say that the Franciscan friars, through their unselfish endeavors, planted the seed of civilization on Texas soil.

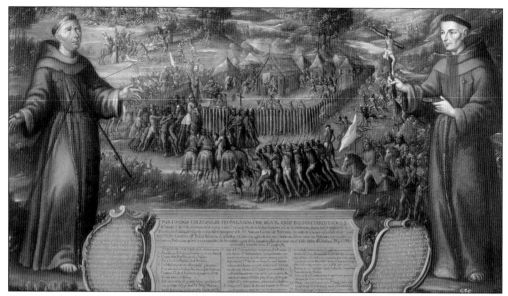

Franciscan missionaries cited the building blocks of what would become cultural centers in Texas, by many means, even by sacrificing their own lives. This is the earliest known painting (1765) by a professional artist of a historical event in Texas. It depicts the destruction of San Sabá Mission and the martyrdom of Fr. Alonso de Terreros and Fr. Joseph Santiesteban.

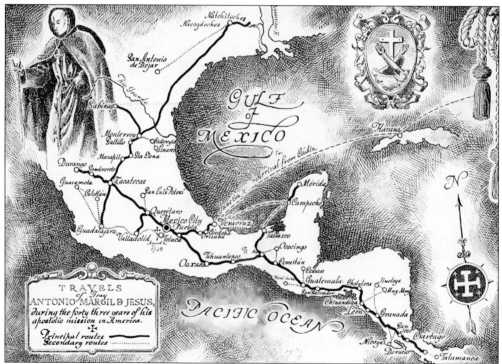

Franciscans, with their rigorous religious culture and virtues, were able to lay the foundations of Texas. This map shows all the travels of Fr. Margil de Jesús from 1683 to 1726. He was able to establish hundreds of missions all over from Costa Rica to Texas and Louisiana by walking thousands of miles, thus receiving the title "The Friar of the Winged Feet."

This is an image of Fr. Antonio Margil de Jesús at the Apostolic College of Guadalupe. He was born in Valencia, Spain, on August 18, 1657. On April 22, 1673, he received the Franciscan habit at La Corona de Cristo in Valencia. He departed Spain on March 4, 1683, and arrived at Veracruz on June 6 where he was assigned to the missionary College of Santa Cruz de Querétaro. After his missionary work in Costa Rica, Nicaragua, Yucatán, and Guatemala, he returned to Mexico to establish the College of Nuestra Señora de Guadalupe in Zacatecas (1707). From there, he set out to establish missions in Coahuila, Nuevo León, and Texas. He spent almost the last years of his life in Texas, from 1716 to 1722, where he founded Guadalupe Mission at Nacogdoches (1716), Dolores Mission near San Augustine (1717), Los Adaes Mission near Robeline (1717), San José and San Miguel de Aguayo Mission on the San Antonio River (1720), and Nuestra Señora del Espíritu Santo Mission near Lavaca Bay (1721). He is considered "the Apostle of Texas."

No one did more to spread the Gospel in New Spain than Fr. Antonio Margil de Jesús, who titled himself and signed every letter as *La Misma Nada* ("Nothingness Itself"). Pictured here, Franciscans in Guadalupe, Zacatecas still keep the remaining belongings that Father Margil used in his missionary travels: his habit, sandals, staff, breviary, gourd of water, and the sacred vessels to celebrate Mass.

Father Margil died in St. Francis Church in Mexico City on August 6, 1726, where he was buried. His remains were twice exhumed, first placed in 1861 at the Cathedral of Mexico City and finally came to rest in 1983 at Guadalupe Friary in Zacatecas, where they can be venerated, as pictured. He was declared venerable by Pope Gregory XVI in July 1836, and his beatification is still in process.

San Antonio de Valero Mission is most commonly known as the site of the Battle of the Alamo (1836). The mission was founded in May 1718 by Father Antonio de San Buenaventura y Olivares of the College of Santa Cruz of Querétaro. It was built from the material of the declining mission of San Francisco Solano, founded in 1700 near the right bank of the Rio Grande at the present site of Guerrero, Coahuila. In 1773, the Franciscans of Querétaro transferred its administration to the Franciscans of Guadalupe, Zacatecas. Below, the mission is in use as a US Army depot in 1868. (Both, courtesy of the San Antonio Conservation Society Foundation.)

San José y San Miguel de Aguayo Mission was founded on February 23, 1720, by Fr. Antonio Margil de Jesús of the College of Guadalupe of Zacatecas. The main church, which is still standing, was constructed in 1768. Known as the "Queen of the Missions," this is the largest of the missions in San Antonio and was almost fully restored in the 1930s. Since that time, Franciscans from the Sacred Heart Province of the United States began to serve the missions. Below, a friar stands in the doorway to the sacristy, and debris from the collapsed roof rests against the left wall in 1928. (Both, courtesy of the San Antonio Conservation Society Foundation.)

San Francisco de la Espada Mission was the first mission in Texas, founded in 1690 as San Francisco de los Tejas near Weches. On March 5, 1731, it was transferred to the San Antonio River area and renamed by Fr. Pedro Muñoz of the College of Santa Cruz of Querétaro.

San Juan Capistrano Mission was founded on July 10, 1716, by Fr. Isidro Félix de Espinosa of the College of Santa Cruz of Querétaro. The mission was originally named San José de los Nazonis Mission and was located in East Texas. After it was abandoned, the mission was renamed and relocated to its present site on March 5, 1731.

Nuestra Señora de la Purísima Concepción de Acuña Mission was originally named Nuestra Señora de la Purísima Concepción de los Hainais and established in the site of present Douglass, in East Texas on July 7, 1716, by Fr. Isidro Félix de Espinosa. On March 5, 1731, the mission was moved to the east bank of the San Antonio River by Fr. Gabriel de Vergara and was renamed in honor of viceroy Juan de Acuña. In 1773, its administration was transferred to the Franciscans of Guadalupe, Zacatecas. Below, a friar walks across the open area behind the south facade of the church in 1929. (Both, courtesy of the San Antonio Conservation Society Foundation.)

The missionary work of the Franciscans in Texas was oriented mainly to protect, help, and educate the Indigenous people. Photograph taken in 1919 of a friar standing by a doorway in Concepción Mission. Traces of frescoes painted by Native American artists can be seen above the door. (Courtesy of the San Antonio Conservation Society Foundation.)

The colonization and Christianization of Texas are some of the great achievements of the Franciscans, obtained through sacrifices, unwavering faith, and limitless patience. This photograph taken in 1921 is of a friar standing next to the baptismal font of Concepción Mission. (Courtesy of the San Antonio Conservation Society Foundation.)

At the beginning of the 1800s, in a major colonizing effort along the Rio Grande, *visitas*, chapels built in remote places, were visited by the Franciscans for the celebration of sacraments. Among these *visitas* were Nuestra Señora de los Dolores in Zapata, La Purísima Concepción in Starr County, and San Agustín in Laredo, here pictured.

After the annexation of Texas to the United States in 1845, most of the Franciscans had returned to Mexico. Secular clergy became in charge of the evangelization. The missionary work was continued mostly by priests of the Oblates of Mary Immaculate Congregation. The Cavalry of Christ, Oblates, priests who visited the missions on horseback, pictured here, served in East and South Texas.

Two

Saints Francis and James Province

The Order of Friars Minor, spread throughout the world, is divided by provinces. To date, there are seven provinces in the United States (a pending project is to unite six of them into one) and there are five Provinces in Mexico. The Franciscans who came to Hebbronville belonged to the Saints Francis and James Province of Mexico. Its Curia headquarters is located in Zapopan, Jalisco, thus, it is known worldwide as the Jalisco Province. It is recognized as the largest Province, having the most friars in the whole Order.

Heirs of five centuries of tradition, culture, and spirituality, the Province of Jalisco feels blessed by the great Heavenly Father, who has carried out his work through the Franciscan friars in these lands of New Spain, today Mexico and part of southwestern United States. Over the centuries, due to political conflicts and anticlerical measures, the Franciscan structure was modified.

The new Province of Saints Francis and James in Mexico was formed on March 19, 1908, from the remains of the Saint Francis Province of Zacatecas, founded in 1604; the Saint James Province of Jalisco, founded in 1607; the Apostolic College of Propaganda Fide of Guadalupe in Zacatecas, founded in 1707; the novitiate of the Apostolic College of Guadalupe that temporarily moved to the San Luis Rey Mission in California since 1892; the Apostolic College of Propaganda Fide of Zapopan in Jalisco, founded in 1816; and the Friary of the Immaculate Conception in Aguascalientes, which belonged to the Province of Saint Diego, founded in 1664. The province has jurisdiction in the following Mexican states: Jalisco, San Luis Potosí, Aguascalientes, Zacatecas, Tamaulipas, Coahuila, Nuevo León, Colima, Durango, and Nayarit; it is aboard in Sienna and Rome, Italy; Corozal, Belize; and in the United States in Hebbronville, Texas.

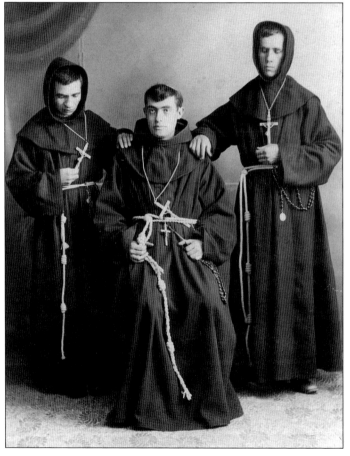

The Franciscan Order in Mexico has its origins when 12 Franciscan missionaries, also known as the "12 Apostles of Mexico," arrived in New Spain on May 13, 1524. After several years of unceasing evangelization work, by the late XVI century, the Franciscan structure in Mexico consisted of five provinces and six Apostolic Colleges. Unfortunately, by the middle of the XIX century, political conflicts and anti-clerical legislations, made it almost impossible for the Franciscans to continue their mission. Most of them had to flee their friaries. Above, seated on the right side, Fr. Teófilo del Sagrado Corazón, a member of the Apostolic College of Zapopan, found refuge with his family. Below, seated is Fr. Agustín Mojica with exiled friars from Zapopan.

In order to revitalize the Franciscan Order in Mexico after all the political conflicts of March 19, 1908, general minister Fr. Dionysius Schüler formed three new provinces in Mexico. One of them was the Saints Francis and James. It merged the Saint James Province of Jalisco; the Saint Francis Province of Zacatecas; the Apostolic College Guadalupe in Zacatecas; the Apostolic College of Zapopan in Jalisco; the Friary of the Immaculate Conception in Aguascalientes, which belonged to the Province of Saint Diego; and the novitiate of the Apostolic College of Guadalupe, which had temporarily moved to the San Luis Rey Mission in California. This is a unique picture taken in 1912 of San Luis Rey Mission. Pictured is the first group of Franciscan novices, who represent the bright future of the recently formed Province of Saints Francis and James.

The St. James Province in Jalisco was founded on February 17, 1607. Its curia was installed in the St. Francis Friary in Guadalajara, Jalisco pictured above. In the beginning, it had 30 friaries. It started to grow with the missionary work of Fr. Juan Larios, who founded several missions in the northern part of the Coahuila Province. The Franciscans commonly built a school and a hospital for the native people, next to the friary. Most of them still remain although they now belong to the secular clergy. By 1900, the province only had the friaries of Guadalajara, Sayula, Santa Anita, Etzatlán, and Asientos. Below is a picture of the last members of the province.

The St. Francis Province in Zacatecas was founded in 1604. Its curia was installed in the St. Francis Friary in Zacatecas, pictured above. By 1736, it had 54 houses founded all over the northern part of Mexico in the states of Tamaulipas, Nuevo León, Chihuahua, Durango, and San Luis Potosí. Although the Apostolic College of Guadalupe was built in 1707 near the curia, both entities were independent and had their own missions. By the end of the 1800s, the province only had the houses of Zacatecas, Somberete, San Luis Potosí, and Durango. At right is a photograph of the last members of the province.

The Apostolic College of Propaganda Fide of Our Lady of Guadalupe in Zacatecas, pictured above, was founded on January 12, 1707, by Fr. Antonio Margil de Jesús. It was the most famous of all the Apostolic Colleges in Mexico. Franciscans from this college used to be prepared to be specialized missionaries for the northern part of New Spain, which later became part of Mexico and the United States. They founded a hospice in Nuevo Leon and over 10 missions in present-day Texas. They established 15 missions in the Mexican state of Tamaulipas and 20 missions in the states of Chihuahua, Durango, and Nayarit. Below, the last Franciscans from the Guadalupe College at the San Luis Rey Mission in California after they were exiled are pictured.

This Apostolic College is an architectural treasure. Most of the buildings are now owned by the Mexican government since the exclaustration during Mexico's War of Reform. The Franciscans only kept possession of the church, the Sanctuary Basilica, dedicated to Our Lady of Guadalupe; to the right is a picture from the interior. Since 1953, the friary hosts the novitiate of the new Jalisco Province. The city of Guadalupe, Zacatecas, developed around the friary, and since its foundation, people have worked together with Franciscans. The picture below is proof of the community assisting the Franciscans with their laundry.

The Apostolic College of Propaganda Fide of Our Lady of Zapopan in Jalisco was founded in 1816 by Franciscans from the Apostolic College of Guadalupe. It started during the time of another political conflict, but in spite of the turmoil, within a few years, the missions were established in the state of Nayarit. The name "Zapopan" derives from Tzapopan, the name of the indigenous peoples who populated the region since around the 12th century. A Spanish expedition led by Nuño Beltrán de Guzmán first came upon the Tzapopan people in 1530. The first Franciscan missionaries brought a small image of Our Lady of the Immaculate Conception to this area and gave her the name of Our Lady of Zapopan. After a few years, the new Province of Saints Francis and James was formed. It became the motherhouse that hosts the curia headquarters and a seminary for Franciscan students.

On December 8, 1541, Fr. Antonio de Segovia gave to the newly settled colony of Zapopan this small image of the Blessed Virgin Mary. In 1653, the bishop of Guadalajara, Juan Ruiz Colmenero, issued a decree declaring the image "miraculous." The image of Our Lady of Zapopan is curated by the Franciscans of the Jalisco Province as their patroness.

The friary complex building in Zapopan is one of the few architectural treasures that was kept by the Franciscans, as it was not confiscated by the government. Since the creation of the Jalisco Province, this building houses the largest friary, and it has been used as a seminary, as pictured.

The construction of the Immaculate Conception Friary in Aguascalientes began in the mid-17th century to about 1651. It was to be part of a convent for the Carmelite order. However, the order did not settle in the village, allowing the priest Pedro Rincón de Ortega, its benefactor, to request that the Franciscans of the San Diego Province take charge of the church and convent. This occurred about 1664. The building is an outstanding example of the Baroque architecture of Aguascalientes, as seen in these interior and exterior photographs. The Franciscans of San Diego served in the town and its surrounding communities for over two centuries.

San Luis Rey, named after Saint Louis IX, the king of France and patron of the Secular Franciscan Order, was one of the last California missions founded on June 13, 1798, by Fr. Fermín de Francisco Lasuén, successor of Saint Junípero Serra. In 1828, the mission was abandoned during Mexico's War of Reform, and on May 12, 1893, it was used as a seminary for the novices and students from the Apostolic College of Guadalupe, pictured here in 1896. The mission belonged to the new Province of Jalisco when it was created, but in 1912, it was given to the St. Barbara Province of the United States.

When the Province of Saints Francis and James was erected in 1908, a total of 18 friaries with a membership of 67 Franciscan friars, less than 10 seminarians, and 7 newly arrived Franciscan friars from Spain composed the province. Pictured is the crowing of Our Lady of Zapopan as patroness of the province.

This is a picture of the first governing body of the recently formed Province of Jalisco. In the center is Msgr. Miguel María de la Mora, bishop of San Luis Potosi; seated from right to left are Fr. Luis del Refugio de Palacio, Fr. Pascual González. Fr. José María Casillas, Fr. Manuel Muñoz, Fr. Nicolás Fernández, and Fr. Juan Gallegos.

Despite the conflict of the Mexican Revolution in 1910, the province survived and vocations flourished. In this picture, Monsignor De la Mora is seated along with the first three Franciscans who arrived in Hebbronville to the right side of him, from left to right: Fr. Guadalupe Torres, Fr. Bernardino Madueño, and Fr. Pascual Ruiz. They are surrounded by young candidates of religious life in San Luis Potosi in 1925.

Shortly after the Mexican Revolution of 1910, there were a few years of prosperity, but they were short-lived. In 1926, President Calles enacted a law that brought conflict and persecution into the lives of the Franciscans. (Chapters three and five will detail these events.) This picture was taken after the exile of Franciscans to Hebbronville. This is a group of students in Zapopan with their teachers Father Cisneros on the center and Father Romero on his right side.

Because of the religious persecution beginning with the Calles Law, by 1929, the province had only five friaries in addition to the one in Hebbronville and a total of 59 friars. By 1934, three more friaries were opened but the number of friars decreased to 46. On April 29, 1936, ex-president Calles was exiled, and with his departure, his political influence was eradicated from Mexico; with this, times of peace and freedom came to the Roman Catholic Church in Mexico. The Franciscan friars gradually returned from Hebbronville to Mexico. In these pictures are former Scotus College students Fathers Cueto, Mora, Luna, Quevedo, Cisneros, Ramirez, and Romero, among others, who returned to Mexico.

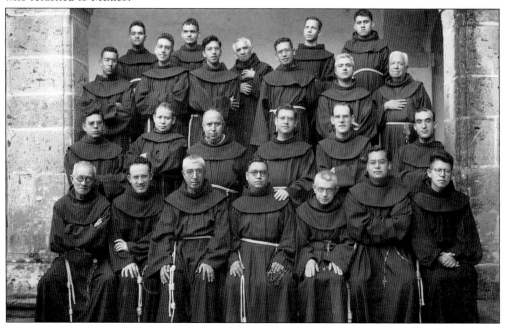

With the return of the Franciscan friars from Hebbronville, the organization of the Saints Francis and James Province started to strengthen. On April 14, 1934, the Holy See confirmed the territorial jurisdiction of the province, which included the Mexican states of Aguascalientes, Coahuila, Colima, Durango, Jalisco, Nayarit, Nuevo León, San Luis Potosí, Sinaloa, Sonora, Tamaulipas, and Zacatecas as well as Baja California and Hebbronville, Texas. Those Franciscan friars who received their entire spiritual and academic formation in the Scotus College in Hebbronville became the future pillars of the province. Fr. Felipe de Jesús Cueto who received his priesthood formation and was ordained in Hebbronville was elected commissioner provincial in 1942. This is a picture taken in Zapopan, Jalisco on September 21, 1951, when the general minister of the Franciscan Order granted the Ordinary Government to the Province of Jalisco. Fr. Felipe de Jesús Cueto became the first provincial minister, pictured here in the center of second row. After being elected general definitor in 1952, Father Cueto was appointed the first bishop of the Diocese of Tlalnepantla in 1964.

When Father Cueto was elected general definitor, Fr. Bernardino Mora became the second provincial minister in 1952. During the mandate of these two Scotus College graduates, the province founded new friaries in San Agustin; Tlaquepaque and Ciudad Guzman in Jalisco; Durango and San Pedro Garza García in Nuevo León; Saltillo, Monclova, and Torreón in Coahuila; and some other friaries in Baja California and Sonora. Besides the increase in number of houses, the number of friars and vocations also started to grow. In the picture above is a group of novices in 1951 in Zapopan, with Father Cueto as provincial minister, seated in the middle on the first row, and to his right side, Father Quevedo, guardian of the friary. Below is the group of philosophy students.

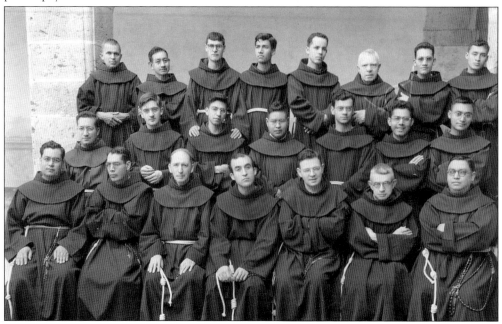

In 1951, the Holy See asked the province to do missionary work with natives in the Sierra of El Nayar, once administered by the Franciscans from the Apostolic College of Guadalupe and the Jesuit fathers. On October 28, 1953, the Santa Clara Mission of Huicholes was founded by Fr. Jose Mercado, pictured above in the third row, fourth from the left. Father Mercado studied at the Scotus College and then was assigned pastor of Hebbronville in 1957. On January 13, 1962, the Prelature of Jesús María del Nayar was erected. Pictured below in the second row, first from left, Fr. Manuel Romero, another student from the Scotus College and former pastor in Hebbronville, was appointed as its first bishop.

By the beginning of the 1960s, the province assumed the spiritual and academic formation of the children and youth by directing and administering the following private schools: Colegio Margil in Aguascalientes, Colegio México in Ciudad Guzmán, Colegio Junípero Serra in Ensenada, Instituto Durango in Durango, Colegio and Escuela Normal in Etzatlán, Colegio Gante in San Pedro Garza García, and Colegio Santa Anita in Jalisco. By 1964, the province had 31 friaries, 366 friars, and 234 students and seminarians. Former Scotus College students here pictured helped in the development of the province: Fathers Cueto, Quevedo, Mora, Romero, Cisneros, Barragán, Hernández, Ramírez, Zaragoza, Solano, Navarro, Palacios, and Muñoz, among others. They are still remembered.

When the religious persecution ceased, the students from the Scotus College returned to Mexico, and new seminaries were established to prepare the new province's vocations. In 1929, the Postulancy was moved from Sarita, Texas to Aguascalientes, then it was moved to Santa Anita, and finally, in the 1960s, to San Agustín, Jalisco. In 1941, the novitiate moved from Hebbronville to Zapopan and on August 13, 1953, it was established in the legendary Apostolic College of Guadalupe, Zacatecas. In 1944, the philosophy faculty moved from the Scotus College to Zapopan, and finally, in 1952, the theology faculty moved to San Pedro Garza García, Nuevo León. Above is a group of novices, and below is a group of philosophy students in Zapopan.

These pictures were taken in Zapopan in the late 1960s when groups of friars gathered for spiritual retreat and formation. With the influence of the Second Vatican Council, a renovation was brought to the province with new legislation and more friaries to be open where the Franciscan presence was required. In 1979, Pope Saint John Paul II visited the Zapopan Basilica. In 1993 the new Province of Junípero Serra was organized from the Jalisco Province, taking the friaries of Sinaloa, Sonora, and Baja, California. Like a phoenix that emerged from the ashes, the Province of Saints Francis and James has developed and grown to become the largest Franciscan province in the world, with 58 friaries, 452 friars (of which 4 are bishops), 271 priests, 3 deacons, 72 brothers, and 137 students and seminarians.

Three

RELIGIOUS PERSECUTION IN MEXICO

Although Mexico is a predominantly Catholic country, the conflict between church and state had begun in the mid-19th century as the Enlightenment ideas of liberalism became enshrined in the Constitution of 1857 headed by Pres. Benito Juarez. The resulting conflict between the secular and ecclesiastical became one of many factors that led to the 1910 Revolution. The new Constitution of 1917 by Venustiano Carranza contained several articles that reduced the political, social, and economic power of the church. But it was Pres. Plutarco Elías Calles who applied the anti-Catholic laws stringently throughout the country and added his own anti-Catholic legislation. In June 1926, he signed the "Law for Reforming the Penal Code", known unofficially as the "Calles Law." This provided specific penalties for priests and religious who dared to violate the provisions of the 1917 Constitution.

In response to these measures, Catholic organizations began to intensify their resistance. On July 11, 1926, the Mexican bishops voted to suspend all public worship in Mexico in response to the Calles Law. In September, the episcopate submitted a proposal for the amendment of the constitution, but this was rejected by Congress on September 22, 1926. Once the rebellion occurred, however, the high clergy did not provide political direction for the movement and the Vatican was even more cautious, fearing religious repression. Some priests sought refuge in secular homes in urban centers while many others left the country. Leadership was left to the popular movements. The rebellions, led by Soldiers of Christ or the Cristeros, took place mainly in the central and western regions of the country: Michoacán, Jalisco, Guanajuato, and Colima; their battle cry was "¡Viva Cristo Rey!" ("Long live Christ the King").

This religious persecution forced the Franciscans of the Saints Francis and James Province in Jalisco, Mexico, to flee and seek refuge in the United States. The war claimed the lives of more than 90,000 military, Cristeros, and numerous civilians, religious and clergy. Following 1940, enforcement of anticlerical restrictions gradually lessened, but it was not until 1992 that the church was restored as a legal entity in Mexico.

Pres. José Venustiano Carranza, here pictured, who saw the church as an obstacle to social reforms, called an assembly of delegates to draft a new constitution. Thus, the Mexican Constitution of 1917, became an attempt by the government to harshly restrict the influence of the Catholic Church within Mexico. (Public domain.)

This picture was taken on June 14, 1926, when Pres. Plutarco Elías Calles signed the "Law for Reforming the Penal Code" to enforce restrictions against the Catholic Church in Article 130 of the Constitution of 1917. This church-state conflict caused religious persecution and a violent uprising called the Cristero War. (Public domain.)

In response to the anticlerical legislative measures, Catholic organizations began to intensify their resistance. The most important group was the National League for the Defense of Religious Liberty, which was joined by the Mexican Association of Catholic Youth and the Popular Union, a Catholic political party. Shown here are pictures of these groups in their manifestations of protest held in Jalisco and Michoacán. On July 14, Catholic bishops endorsed plans for an economic boycott against the government, and in September 1926, with the support of Pope Pius XI, the Mexican Catholic bishops submitted a proposal to amend the Constitution, but it was rejected by the Mexican Congress on September 22. (Both, public domain.)

Between 1926 and 1929, religious refugees either fled or were deported to the United States, as the Mexican government enforced anticlerical laws that limited the number of priests, dissolved religious orders, and subjected the clergy to direct persecution. Clergy initially left the country voluntarily, choosing self-exile over obeying the restrictions; by early 1927, however, exile was no longer a matter of personal choice. Above, bishop Manuel Azpeitia of Tepic along with his diocesan presbytery arriving in Los Angeles (Courtesy of University of California, Los Angeles.); below, a group of Sisters of the Sacred Heart of Mary arriving in San Antonio (Both, courtesy of Institute of Texan Cultures.)

Although migration from Mexico to the United States had been occurring since the mid-nineteenth century, it was the devastation caused by the Cristero War that reinforced and solidified these trends during the latter part of the 1920s. The unprecedented growth of Mexican communities in Texas, California, and the Southwest, occurring in conjunction with the arrival of the refugees and the closing of Catholic schools in Mexico, generated a concurrent demand for Mexican Catholic schools in the United States. Above, Father José de Jesús Angulo is with a group of nuns teaching children outdoors in Jalisco; below, refugees cross the border of Texas in 1927. (Both, public domain.)

By January 1927, many of the faithful concluded that they had exhausted all peaceful means of protest and the formal rebellion began. The landowning peasant class in the rural west took up arms, they were called Cristeros (Soldiers of Christ). This picture, taken in 1928, shows Cristeros presenting weapons in homage to the Blessed Sacrament in southern Jalisco. (Public domain.)

Due to the Cristeros' lack of military training and supplies, they mostly relied on guerrilla tactics, until they recruited former general, Enrique Gorostieta, to coordinate their efforts. The Mexican episcopate never supported the rebellion; nevertheless, some members of the clergy took part in it. This photograph taken in 1929 shows Cristeros celebrating Holy Mass outdoors in Huejuquilla, Jalisco. (Public domain.)

A courageous minority of priests refused to leave the country. They went into hiding and roamed the towns and countryside by night and in disguise, doing their best to bring the sacraments to the faithful. If caught, they were arrested, fined, jailed, and sometimes tortured and executed. Public worship was a crime punishable by hanging or firing squad. Twenty-five Mexican saints and martyrs who remained true to their faith during these turbulent years were canonized by Pope John Paul II in 2000. Another 13 martyrs were canonized by Pope Benedict XVI in 2005. Above, Cristeros are hung on utility poles in Zapotlán, Jalisco; below, Fr. Francisco Vera is executed by firing squad after celebrating Mass in 1927. (Both, public domain.)

Fr. Miguel Agustín Pro, a Jesuit priest, was executed in Mexico City on November 23, 1927, without the benefit of a trial. President Calles invited the press to photograph the execution. Declining a blindfold, he knelt in prayer, he faced and blessed his executioners with a crucifix in one hand and a rosary in the other. Before the firing squad was ordered to shoot, he raised his arms in the shape of a cross and shouted "¡Viva Cristo Rey!" When the firing squad shots failed to kill him, a soldier administered a coup de grâce that ended his life. He was beatified by Pope John Paul II in 1988. (Both, public domain.)

Four

HEBBRONVILLE, TEXAS

The history of the region starts with the Villas del Norte settlements of Reynosa, Camargo, Revilla, Mier, and Laredo established by José de Escandón between 1740 and 1755 and the Spanish and Mexican land grants that were issued to families in the late 1700s and early 1800s. Present-day Hebbronville sits on one of the original Spanish land grants, Las Noriecitas, that was granted to Don Simon de Ynojosa in 1740. Heirs of the Ynojosa family sold a portion to Francisco P. Peña, who established Peña Station, a stop on the Texas Mexican Railway line between Corpus Christi and Laredo. When Peña refused to sell the land for a townsite, the railway company made arrangements with James Hebbron to purchase land just west of Peña Station that would become the location of the new railroad depot. The town of Hebbronville developed around the new location. The present community of Hebbronville was the scene of extensive ranching, which was the reason for the development of the town. The ranches to the south drove their herds to the depot to ship them north to markets as far away as Kansas. Eventually, Hebbronville became the largest cattle shipping point in the United States.

In 1913, Jim Hogg County was formed from portions of Brooks, Starr, Duval, and Zapata Counties and was named after James Hogg, the 20th governor of Texas. Hebbronville still remains the county seat. The county was designated the Vaquero capital of Texas in 2005 and honors the heritage of the ranching industry with county fairs and festivals. The population of the county remains at approximately 5,000. In addition to ranching, Jim Hogg County is also known as one of the premier areas for dove, quail, and white-tailed deer hunting.

The first settlers of the region were primarily Catholic and the first church was built in 1898 by Fr. Miguel Puig, who foresaw the development of Hebbronville and began to travel from Aguilares to administer Sacraments. Twenty-eight years later, the Franciscans would arrive, build the Scotus College, and still reside to this day for the spiritual, cultural, and educational care of this community.

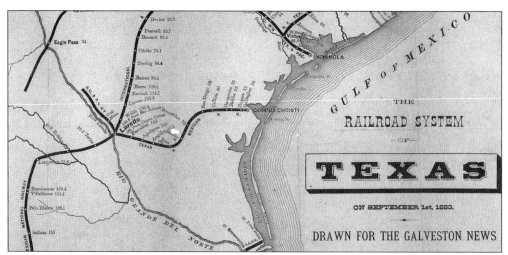

Before the founding of Hebbronville, the region was occupied by Native Americans and wild mustangs, giving the region the name "Llanos Mesteños." Gradually, the land was settled through Spanish and Mexican land grants, and in 1881, the Texas-Mexico Railway was built to connect the port of Corpus Christi to the border town of Laredo. The railroad dipped slightly south to reach a dray station and a small community owned by Francisco Peña before continuing to Laredo. It became known as Peña Station and remained in operation for several years. It was the southernmost railroad station for travelers to the region and from the ranches to the south to points north. Below is a picture of the Peña family taken in 1890.

When Peña did not want to sell his land for a townsite, the Texas Mexican Railway made arrangements with James R. Hebbron, pictured here. The town was laid out in 20 blocks of 12 lots each, and the new town was named Hebbronville. The depot was loaded onto a flat car and moved 1.5 miles west, where it still sits today.

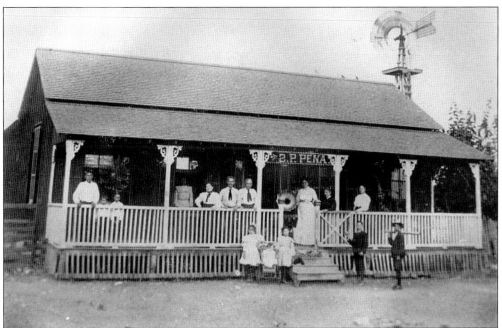

The Peña family were some of the first merchants in Hebbronville along with F.B. Guerra and S. E. Garcia supplying the town's people and ranches with much-needed supplies that were brought in by rail. Narciso Peña was the first postmaster.

The Hebbronville Depot was a bustling and thriving center of activity, as it was the best mode of transportation and the supply line for goods and supplies. Existing roads wound through private ranch lands containing many gates and were hard to travel, as they were either deep sand or very rocky land—both very difficult for wagons and the first cars. In 1906, the first telegraph line was established connecting Hebbronville to the outside world and making contact with cattle markets much more reliable. Shipping pens were built just east of the depot, where the many ranches to the south would drive their cattle to load on cattle cars bound for the livestock markets as far away as Kansas City. Hebbronville was considered the most important business area north of Rio Grande City and south of San Antonio. Eventually, Hebbronville became the largest cattle shipping point in the United States as the cattle industry grew and prospered.

In 1913, Jim Hogg County was formed out of portions of Brooks, Duval, and other neighboring counties and was named for Gov. James Hogg, the first Texas-born governor of Texas. This is a picture of his family taken around 1890.

The Jim Hogg County Court House and jail were built in 1913 and Hebbronville was named the county seat by a unanimous vote of 176 giving the town its hub of government. The stately building also served as the meeting place for church services and other organizations.

The Jim Hogg County Court House has continued to serve as the seat of county government. The building is still in use to hold the district courtroom, the offices of the county judge and the county clerk, and the commissioners court.

The first grand jury was convened in 1913, here pictured. The town was incorporated in 1930. However, the economic crush of the Great Depression caused financial hardship and the voters decided to dissolve the city's charter on February 1, 1932.

The Hotel Viggo was built in 1915 by C.F. Luque for the owner, Viggo Kohler. A few years later, the south wing was added by Joseph Gruy. Perfectly situated between Corpus Christi and Laredo and between San Antonio and the Rio Grande Valley, it served many travelers and was a refuge for area ranchers when threatened by marauding bandits. With beautiful architecture and large second- and third-floor screened porches, the hotel served many guests and offered a full-service restaurant. Located conveniently just across the street from the courthouse, it served as accommodations for businessmen. A number of famous guests were hosted there through the years, and it served the community for club meetings, business meetings, and parties.

The first and foremost industry in Jim Hogg County was the cattle industry. The region was settled by Spanish and Mexican land grantees who moved north from the communities of Mier, Camargo, and Guerrero and established their large ranches. Hebbronville was the hub for supplies and shipping cattle to market via the railroad. Ranches were not just places of business but also social gatherings. Neighboring ranches helped each other with working cattle and then enjoyed social time after the work was done. The ranching families and their guests enjoyed picnics, games, food, and music together. Many of the original land grantees still own and operate their family lands, passing them down from generation to generation.

The first cattle in the area were the hardy longhorn cattle well-suited to the dry and harsh conditions of the region. After the Civil War, the industry began to flourish. Cattle drives moved the cattle to markets to the north as the demand for beef increased. This was the era of the Chisolm Trail and the great cattle drives from Texas to Kansas. When the railroad was established in Hebbronville, cattle shipping pens were built. The many ranches to the south drove their cattle herds to load on the cattle cars, making the reach to markets much easier. The railroad made it more economical to produce and sell cattle.

As the demand for beef increased, other breeds of cattle were introduced such as the heavier Hereford. In the following decades, breeds such as the Brahma, Beefmaster, Santa Gertrudis, and Angus were introduced. None of the ranches would have been able to thrive had it not been for the contribution of vaqueros, traditional Mexican cowboys who had all the skills and knew all the methods for handling horses and cattle. Their talents extended into managing water and fencing and producing hand-made saddles and tack and other tools needed for the trade.

The Old Garza House, the oldest house in Hebbronville, was built in 1893 by Don Bonifacio Garza. Also known as "Casa de Cuatro Aguas," the house served as Hebbronville's post office for a few years. In 1898, the house was sold to Jose Angel Garza, a community pioneer and entrepreneur. This home provided sanctuary for Capuchin Poor Clares nuns exiled during Mexico's Cristero War of the 1920s.

In the early 1930s, the number of students in the local schools had doubled, requiring more classrooms and faculty. A new high school was built in 1937, pictured here, and in 1951, it was greatly expanded. The old building was later remodeled and became the district's grade school.

In 1914, the first theater in Hebbronville, the Casino Theater, was established by Patricio Cruz. The building, located across the street from the town plaza, was used for theatrical plays, high school commencement exercises, wedding receptions, and other social functions of those days. The building still stands today.

By the mid-1920s, Hebbronville was thriving with commerce. There were dry goods stores, as well as bakeries, a shoe shop, hardware and feed stores, a bank, a car dealership, the electric and telephone companies, the water company, and more, all fed by the cattle industry and the newly discovered oil fields of nearby Mirando City and Thompsonville.

As the town grew, more businesses were added along the main street. Extending down a five-block area, the unnamed street was simply called "Main Street." However, when the streets were named, it became Galbraith Avenue. Even so, the citizens still referred to it as Main Street, mostly identifying locations by landmarks.

Organized in 1913, the First State Bank was located in a simple building just off Main Street. By 1926, with increased capital raised, it was converted to the First National Bank of Hebbronville, and a new building was erected on the main street now known as Galbraith Avenue.

One of Hebbronville's most beloved businesses and biggest attractions was the popular Frank's Cafe established by Francisco Gutierrez Sr. in 1921. Originally a general store named "El Precio Fijo," the family turned the store into a restaurant in 1938. Frank's Cafe (also known as Paco's) continued the family tradition with its delicious food, casual, friendly atmosphere, and unique charm.

All the first businesses of Hebbronville were small family-owned businesses and often offered more than one service. A barbershop may also sell gasoline or offer shoe repair while a drugstore may also serve food. Enterprising business owners existed to serve the community, whatever the need. Many businesses were passed down from generation to generation, and some still exist today.

The historic New York Store was established in 1909 by Sixto Garcia, one of the first merchants in Hebbronville. The original building was located at Peña Station, but in 1929, it was relocated to Galbraith Street. At first, it served as a general store, providing the community with groceries, hardware, and agriculture supplies and equipment. Over the years, the store provided tailoring, alterations, and cleaning and pressing services and expanded its Western wear department.

One of the most needed businesses was the dry goods store. Jose A. Garza owned the General Merchandise Store and sold food, hardware, kerosene, and many household items. A gas pump outside provided needed fuel for the few cars in town. His descendants still operate Central Furniture Store in the same location.

The newly built Piggly Wiggly grocery store was the most modern store in the 1930s and 1940s. Upstairs were offices including a dentist's office. Although the store was a symbol of progress and town growth, it was not unusual to see a horse tied up in front, as many old ways were still in play.

The old main street (pictured in a view looking west) in the 1920s and 1930s still had the flavor of an Old West town built on the prairie. Cowboys still rode their horses to town but modern conveniences were making life easier and trips to town on a Saturday were a treat and an opportunity for shopping and socializing.

The Texas Theater, built on the corner of Galbraith Avenue and Highway 16, came to town in 1935 and was touted as being a modern fire-proof building. It was operated by the Long Theater Company. However, it burned to the ground in 1953, and Long Theater built El Rancho Theater on the same site. Western movies of the day were the most popular films, and the El Rancho showed the newest movies as they came out. The El Rancho was the hub of entertainment, enjoyed by people of all ages, and a great place for children for Saturday matinees, for individuals, and for couples for date nights. It kept the citizens of the area connected to the outside world, the newest movies, their favorite stars, and news reels. Eventually, the manager, Al Knoppe, retired. The theater was now old and irreparable and was torn down.

When Hebbronville was platted and lots sold, Catholics living in and around Peña Station were the first ones to buy these lots. Fr. Miguel Puig, pictured above, foresaw the development of Hebbronville and began to travel from Aguilares to administer Sacraments. On June 13, 1898, Father Puig began to construct the first chapel with the help of Silvestre Gutierrez, James McGovern, and Narciso Peña. The chapel was completed on October 19, 1899, and was dedicated to St. Isidore. In 1922, the chapel was instituted as Parish of Hebbronville.

When Father Puig was transferred to Laredo in 1899, Hebbronville remained without a priest for three years. Finally, in 1902, Fr. A. Serra took over the next seven months until Fr. E.M. de Buyn traveled occasionally from San Diego to Hebbronville. In 1922, Fr. L. Cunningham, became the first pastor until 1925. In that year, Fr. Juan Bautista Lavaie, pictured above, took over and made some improvements. His term lasted until 1926 when he turned over the church to the Franciscan friars when they arrived in Hebbronville. It was Bishop Emmanuel Boleslaus Ledvina, pictured at right, of the Diocese of Corpus Christi, who gladly received the Franciscans and offered them the Parish of Hebbronville.

This is a panoramic view of Hebbronville from the balcony of the Hotel Viggo about 1915 looking east. The courthouse, built in 1913, faced south and sat at the heart of the town surrounded by businesses on Main Street just one block south, the hotel to its west, and residences all around. Directly behind the courthouse to the north was the new jail and sheriff's office. As there were not yet city services, the water was supplied by a well and windmill. The first school building was behind the courthouse, and there was a stock pen for the sheriff's horses. Directly behind was the original St. Isidore Catholic Church showing above the roof of the courthouse. In 1981, construction on a new west wing in the courthouse was begun, enlarging the district clerk and treasurer's offices, remodeling the district courtroom, and providing additional office space for other county officials.

Five

FRANCISCAN PRESENCE IN HEBBRONVILLE

The religious persecution by the Mexican government made it impossible for the Franciscan friars to live in peace. Fr. Antonio María Gómez, who was the commissioner of the Saints Francis and James Franciscan Province, appointed three priests to establish a religious house in South Texas, giving the Franciscans a refuge. The three priests were Frs. Bernardino Madueño, Guadalupe Torres, and Pascual Ruiz.

In June 1926, Father Madueño traveled to Laredo, San Antonio, and El Paso to ask the bishops from these dioceses for refuge. None of them offered shelter. On August 4, Father Madueño traveled to Corpus Christi and had an interview with its Bishop Emmanuel B. Ledvina, who gladly accepted the Franciscans in his diocese and offered the parish in Hebbronville. Bishop Ledvina appointed Father Madueño as its first Franciscan pastor. Fathers Torres and Ruiz, who were in San Antonio, received the good news from Father Madueño, and on August 6, 1926, these three Franciscans arrived in Hebbronville for the first time.

During the first few months of Franciscan presence, the friars saw the necessity to enlarge the church building, which was originally built in 1899. They also envisioned the construction of a seminary, the Scotus College, to receive the Franciscan seminarians and friars of the province, while persecution persisted. But even though hostilities against the Catholic Church ended in 1932, the Franciscans remained in Hebbronville, unlike other religious orders who eventually returned to their homeland, leaving their adoptive homes.

There is no doubt that all the work and effort of the Franciscans resulted in spiritual and cultural growth for the community of Hebbronville and the surrounding areas. Just as drops of water change the surface of a rock over time, it took years for the Franciscans' presence to establish the gift and spirit of their order in the community.

The Council of Franciscans of the Saints Francis and James Province of Mexico in 1926 at the start of the religious persecution. Pictured are (1) Fr. Antonio M. Gómez (commissar), (2) Fr. Antonio J. Ráfago, (3) Fr. Pedro Camacho, (4) Fr. Vicente Macedo, (5) Fr. Guadalupe Torres, and (6) Fr. Daniel Meza (secretary).

Fr. Antonio María Gómez Monraz was born in Teuchitlán, Jalisco, on September 25, 1880. He was a former friar of the Apostolic College of Guadalupe and was elected commissar of the Saints Francis and James Province of Mexico from 1926 to 1935, during the difficult religious persecution period.

Fr. Bernardino de Santa María de Guadalupe Madueño was born in San Gabriel, Jalisco, in 1881. Father Gómez, a commissioner, assigned him the duty of looking for shelter for the Franciscans in South Texas. He was appointed as the first pastor of the Hebbronville Parish by bishop Ledvina of the Diocese of Corpus Christi. He served from 1926 to 1930.

Fr. José Guadalupe Torres was born in Guadalajara, Jalisco, on January 1, 1864. He first served as a diocesan priest in Puerto Vallarta, Jalisco, in 1905. Later, he decided to join the Franciscan Order. When he arrived in Hebbronville, he instructed and fostered the first students of the future Scotus College.

Fr. Pascual Ruiz was born in Espiritu Santo, Zacatecas, in 1893. One of the first students of the new Province of Jalisco, he was sent to California to finish his formation. He was ordained as a priest three years before the persecution began. When he arrived in Hebbronville, he helped with the development of students and the ministries of the parish.

A group of Franciscans from the Cantabria Province of Spain helped in the education of the new seminarians in the Province of Jalisco: Fr. José Román Zulaica, Fr. Jaime Pedro Otálora, Fr. Matías Ortiz de Ortuño, Fr. Jesús Alejaldre, and Fr. Juan Antonio Sesma. Father Otálora, who is pictured here, was the third pastor and guardian from 1931 to 1941.

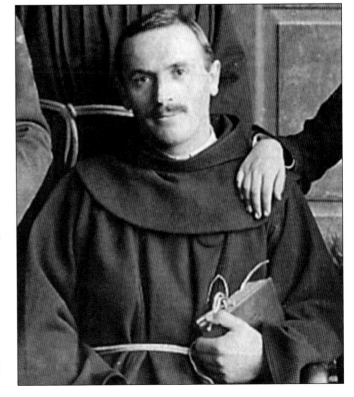

Once the Franciscans arrived in Hebbronville, they had two main tasks: to serve as the administrators of the Parish and instruct the seminarians who had arrived from Mexico. The land granted to the Franciscans was a total of six lots, each measuring 50 by 150 feet. Pictured here is the church with the surrounding lots.

The first house where the Franciscans lived also served as the visiting priest's quarters and the parish office. As seen in the picture, it was only 57 feet by 28 feet with four rooms. The first community of eleven seminarians and four friars managed to live here.

When the Franciscans arrived in Hebbronville, this was the church they encountered. It was built with stone and measured 49 feet by 28 feet. It was Gothic style with a wooden ceiling, and four windows on each side. It had a bell tower in the middle, a second-floor choir, and a small sacristy to the right of the entrance. It was built under the direction of Father Puig. First dedicated to St. Isidore, in November 1922, it was canonically designated as a parish by Monsignor Ledvina. Fr. Leonard Cunningham, a Passionist priest, who was the pastor in San Diego, Texas, would come to Hebbronville to celebrate the Sacraments every week. In 1926, the Franciscans began to administer the parish. In October 1970, this church was demolished, and when the new church was built, the debris was used to fill the basement, which now is directly beneath the parish office.

The original church had two rows of nine wooden pews, two of which are still conserved in the Franciscan Museum of Hebbronville. The original images in the church were St. Isidore in the middle, the Immaculate Conception on the left, and St. Joseph on the right. On two columns on each side, there were the statues of the Sacred Heart of Jesus and St. Anthony of Padua; all of them are still on the actual church. On July 9, 1927, the Franciscans obtained permission from Bishop Ledvina to change the patron saint from St. Isidore to the patroness of Our Lady of Guadalupe. On May 24, 1936, Marie Stella Turcotte Kenedy donated the altar of the church, made of cedar in San Luis Potosí. Part of the original cedar altar is still present in today's church, although it was enlarged.

These were the first Franciscan seminarians who arrived in Hebbronville on August 15, 1926: (1) Fr. Antonio J. Rábago, (2) Fr. Guadalupe Torres, (3) Br. Leonardo Medina, (4) Br. Serafín Barragán, (5) Br. Manuel Jiménez, (6) Br. Ángel Ochoa, (7) Tomás Palacios, (8) Br. Felipe Quevedo, (9) Br. Everardo Velásquez, (10) Br. Conrado Hernández, (11) Br. Jaime Escobar, (12) Br. Buenaventura Hernández, (14) Br. Félix García, and (15) Br. Sebastián de Alba.

The Franciscans founded the Scotus College, a seminary for young men studying to become Franciscan friars and priests. This is the original Scotus College seal. On August 19, 1926, the first group of students started classes. It was not until November 17, 1932, that the Scotus College was officially recognized by the US Department of Education.

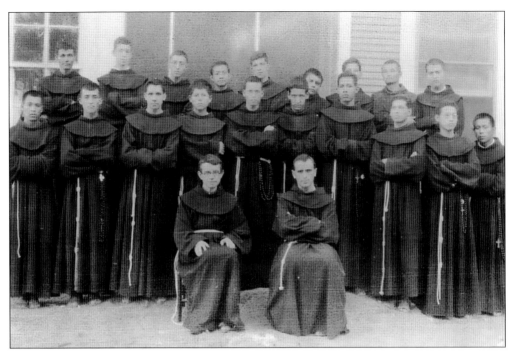

On August 15, 1927, twenty-one young postulants received their Franciscan habit from Fr. Gómez, commissioner. These were the first novices of the new community of Hebbronville. Included in the first image, from left to right, are (first row) Fr. Antonio Gómez, Fr. Pedro J. Otálora, novice master; (second row) Br. Juan Rábago, Br. Buenaventura Sandoval, Br. Bernardino Mora, Br. Raymundo Solano, Br. León Zaragoza, Br. Salvador Navarro, Br. Agustín Ramírez, Br. Felipe de Jesús Cueto, Br. Bernardo García, and Br. Benito Maldonado. The second image shows the whole community of novices, seminarians, and friars in 1927.

The construction work of the Scotus College was carried out primarily by the Franciscan friars. On January 5, 1927, the Franciscans obtained permission from Monsignor Ledvina, who also donated $3,000 to start the construction of the first original building made of wood on the left side of St. Isidore church (above). A few months later, in April 1927, they started to build the structure on the right side of the church with the same material. This structure was to serve as the parish office, classrooms, and a chapel for the novitiate (below).

The first Scotus College building was made of wood. It had two floors of 80 feet by 30 feet each. The walls were 7 inches deep and the ceilings were 33 feet. The building was located on the left side of the current church. Each floor had eight windows facing the front. In total, there were 29 rooms, which were used only for sleeping quarters for the friars. These pictures depict different views of the first wooden building of the Scotus College. It was demolished when the new concrete building was completed.

The extension of the wooden Scotus College was located on the right side of the church and consisted of only one floor of 38 feet by 30 feet. It housed the classrooms and the parish office. By the beginning of May 1927, the construction of the dining room and kitchen started. The space was 47 feet by 23 feet. Above is a view of the Scotus College's cloister and the gardens. Below, Fr. Fernando Cisneros, one of the first novices of Hebbronville and later teacher, is at the entrance of the first Scotus College building.

By 1928, the Franciscan community had grown to 38 friars and new seminarians from Mexico were arriving. Seated from left to right are Fr. Serafín Barragán, Fr. Juan A. Sesma, Fr. Bernardino Madueño, Fr. José R. Zulaca, Fr. Antonio M. Gómez, Fr. Guadalupe Torres, Fr. Matías Otuño, and Fr. Pedro Otálora.

Members of the Franciscan community are pictured in 1938. From left to right, (second row) the first seven friars are Fr. Bernardino Mora, Fr. Ángel Ochoa, Fr. Felipe de Jesús Cueto, Fr. José R. Zulaca, Fr. Pedro Otálora, Fr. Agustín Ramírez, and Fr. Domingo Muñoz; (third row) the first three friars are Br. Gil de la Fuente, Br. Manuel Romero, and Br. Félix García; (fourth row) the first seven friars are Br. Gabriel Mariscal, Br. Felipe López, Br. José Mercado, Br. Ignacio Ramírez, Br. Jesús García, and Br. Rafael Cervantes.

The service of the religious nonclerical friars has always been appreciated. They are responsible for doing the manual work in the sacristy, kitchen, farm, garden, and tailor shop. This is a group of nonclerical brothers in 1938. From left to right, (first row) the second friar is Br. Félix García, the third is Br. Gil de la Fuente, and the fifth is Br. Bernardo García; (second row) the first two friars are Br. Trinidad González and Br. Guadalupe Parra.

With the time and support of the community of Hebbronville, the Franciscans had new vocations that were coming from Mexico despite the religious persecution. The new candidates for religious life, after some months of formation in postulancy, received the Franciscan habit to start the novitiate. These novices of 1938 are pictured with their master, Fr. Bernardino Mora.

Although vocations were increasing, not all persevered. Some seminarians left the religious life and went back to Mexico. By 1935, there were 28 students in philosophy and theology studies. Pictured here are some of these seminarians. The people of Hebbronville were amazed at the development of the seminarians despite the hardships and poverty they endured.

The seminarians also enjoyed a little free time to socialize and have fun. On March 10, 1932, the Franciscans saw snow in Hebbronville for the first time. Students enjoyed a wonderful school day off.

From 1928 through 1939, the seminarians helped in the improvements needed at the Scotus College. Br. Tomás Palacios, with the help of some students, was in charge of the installation of the electrical network for the seminary and the church. The seminarians drilled a well measuring 261 feet deep. A windmill drew water up from the well. They also constructed a seven-foot-high wooden fence around the building. All these improvements and the hard work of the seminarians can be seen in these pictures.

This was the original design for the new Scotus College concrete building in 1940. The plan was presented by Fr. Felipe de Jesús Cueto, who was the guardian. By 1942, many of the seminarians were returning to Mexico, and only the first wing, pictured on the left, was completed.

On March 29, 1940, the construction of the concrete Scotus College building started and was completed in 1944. It was designed by and constructed under the supervision of José Juan Álvarez. The Franciscan friars helped by obtaining financial support with donations and with hours of hard manual work.

Painted white and sitting on a large palm-lined green lawn, the Scotus College's segmental arched linear ambulatory crowning the ridge of its red Spanish tiled roof, is visible for miles beyond the city limits. It is considered a treasure and one of a kind in the entire state of Texas. The large two-story classroom and residential facility housed up to 250 Franciscan seminarians from 1926 to 1952, some of them later became bishops. The Scotus College is the preeminent architectural landmark in Hebbronville, and it was named after the revered Scottish Franciscan theologian from the Middle Ages, John Duns Scotus.

It took a little more than four years to finish the construction of the Scotus College building. Fr. Felipe de Jesús Cueto started the project, but in 1942, he was appointed commissar and then became the first minister provincial of the Saints Francis and James Province. Consequently, Fr. Francisco Luna, pictured, was appointed guardian of the Friary in Hebbronville and finished the construction project. Architect José Juan Álvarez, a Hebbronville resident and experienced contractor, guided the project to the end. Even though in 1941, Fr. José María Casillas, commissioner, decided to take the novitiate back to Mexico, the building project continued. Upon completion, the blessing was held on November 8, 1944, on the feast of Blessed John Duns Scotus by bishop Mariano S. Garriga.

By the beginning of the 1940s, the situation in Mexico was getting better and the religious animosity ceased. It was safer for the Franciscan seminarians to return to their homeland and continue their studies. It was also time to stabilize institutions and restore the Franciscan friaries that had been abandoned during the persecution. In 1942, the faculty of philosophy at Scotus College was moved to Zapopan. In 1952, the last generation of students of theology left the Scotus College and returned to Mexico. The last Franciscans who were ordained in Hebbronville were the priest Octavio Michel Corona, pictured here in the balcony of the Scotus College between the American and Mexican flags, and deacon Lorenzo Flores Delgado on March 8, 1952.

Dominican friars arrived mainly from Spain and were in charge of parishes in San Diego, Falfurrias, and Benavides, near Hebbronville. This picture was taken on Saint Francis of Assisi Feast Day October 4, 1942. Franciscans from Hebbronville are on the left, and Dominicans from San Diego are on the right.

The first Franciscan priests ordained in Hebbronville are pictured. Ordained on September 19, 1930: Fr. Tomás Palacios and Fr. Felipe Quevedo. September 19, 1931: Fr. Ángel Ochoa. September 24, 1932: Fr. Felipe de Jesús Cueto, Fr. Buenaventura Sandoval, Fr. Salvador Navarro, and Fr. Raymundo Solano. October 4, 1933: Fr. Bernardino Mora, Fr. León Zaragoza and Fr. Juan Rábago.

As the first generations of Franciscan friars finished were ordained as priests, they served as guides to the new generations. With the graduation of the men in the Scotus College, the solidification of the Jalisco Province started. The graduates who received their training entirely at Scotus College and were ordained as priests from 1939 to 1942, pictured above from left to right, are Fr. Felipe López, Fr. Fernando Cisneros, Fr. Felipe Quevedo, Fr. Felipe de Jesús Cueto, Fr. Ángel Ochoa, Fr. Agustín Ramírez, and Fr. Domingo Muñoz. The photograph below is of the rest of the community.

The students of theology in 1941 are pictured with their teacher Fr. Agustín Ramírez. Some of the friars recognized in the picture are still remembered by the friars of the Jalisco Province: Br. José Mercado, Br. Ignacio Ramírez, Br. Rafael Cervantes, Br. Gabriel Mariscal, and Br. Jesús García.

When the Franciscans finished their priestly formation in Hebbronville, if they qualified, they were allowed to continue graduate studies in different parts of the country. Pictured are Fr. Felipe de Jesús Cueto (second from left) and Fr. Agustín Ramírez (third from left) with two students in Washington, DC, for studies in the Catholic University of America.

After almost 20 years of Franciscan presence in Hebbronville, the Catholic community grew in numbers. The constant presence of Franciscan priests and their spiritual guidance, the daily celebration of the Sacraments, the education of children and the youth at the parochial school led by nuns, and the many Parish ministry groups guided by the Franciscans all contributed to the increase of the Catholic congregation members in Hebbronville. The small church was not big enough to host the entire community. These pictures show the construction of the new church in the 1950s.

Although the last Franciscan seminarians returned to Mexico in 1952 and Scotus College ceased to function as a seminary, the Franciscans have remained in Hebbronville to the present. They continue the administration and spiritual guidance of Our Lady of Guadalupe Parish. The Franciscans have always been responsible for the maintenance, improvements, and construction of the Scotus College, its offices, and all related church buildings. To the left is Fr. Domingo Muñoz with a contract worker during the construction of the church bell towers in 1952. Below is the interior of the church, prior to the construction of the dome in 1952.

The first stone for the new church of Our Lady of Guadalupe was blessed and laid on September 18, 1946. The construction started a few months later with Fr. Domingo Muñoz as the pastor. The construction lasted over 18 years and several pastors contributed to the project: Fr. Domingo Muñoz (1946–1948 and 1953–1954), Fr. Aloysius Morán (1948–1949), Fr. Juan Rábago (1950–1953), Fr. Manuel Romero (1954–1957), Fr. José Mercado (1957–1959), and Fr. Luis Velásquez (1960–1966). Pictured here is Fr. Domingo Muñoz in his second term as pastor in 1954. He is reviewing the blueprints of the construction of the church with one of the contract workers. The roof was not yet constructed. The main entrance to the church is in the background. Above the entrance are the choir loft and stairs that will lead to the roof and bell towers.

The picture above shows the installed ceiling of the church with the stairs from the choir that led to the roof and the bell towers in 1962. Pictured below from left to right are Fr. Manuel Romero, Fr. Domingo Muñoz, and architect José Juan Álvarez, the designer and building contractor for Scotus College, who also helped the construction team of the new church. This photograph was taken at the main entrance to the church on St. Clara Street in 1962.

In the image to the right, Fr. Manuel Romero Arvizu stands on the roof of the new church, in front of the left bell tower on the west side. Father Romero was the pastor of Our Lady of Guadalupe Parish from 1954 to 1957. Many Hebbronville residents remember his catechism classes. On August 15, 1964, he was ordained as the first bishop of the Prelate of Jesús María del Nayar in Nayarit, Mexico. He was the first Scotus College graduate and the first Franciscan of the new Saints Francis and James Province to be ordained as a bishop. Below is a panoramic view of Hebbronville taken from the roof of the church.

It took effort, financial resources, and time to finish the construction of the new church. With the help of the community, it was officially finished in 1964, with Fr. Luis Velasquez as pastor. The incongruously composed new sanctuary includes a rose-colored Alamoesque parapet flanked by twin towers in front and a golden-tiled dome at the rear. Alluding to the 18th-century Basilica of Guadalupe in Mexico City, the building is more attuned to a Mission Revival style, as seen in this picture taken in 1958. This majestic church with its two towers, its classic cross design, and its beautiful central dome is visible for miles beyond the city limits. The Franciscans still administer the Our Lady of Guadalupe Parish, first as part of the Diocese of Corpus Christi and since 2000 as part of the Diocese of Laredo when it was formed. The Franciscans continue diligently today to be committed to the spiritual formation and care of the Catholic community in Hebbronville.

Six

MISSIONS AROUND
HEBBRONVILLE

With the arrival of the Franciscans to Hebbronville, surrounding communities were also blessed. Along with the Parish in Hebbronville, Bishop Ledvina granted the Franciscans the responsibility to temporally look after various communities near Hebbronville that were located in the Duval, Jim Hogg, and Webb Counties.

These are the words of bishop Ledvina in the contract between the Diocese and the Franciscan Province in 1926:

> The reverend bishop full of sadness by the religious persecution held in Mexico and with all his heart in Christ and Francis, having heard the Diocesan consultants for the canonical foundation and sustention, gives refuge to the Franciscans and grants the right 'in perpetuam' (perpetually) to the Franciscan friars of the Province in Jalisco: the St. Isidore church in Hebbronville and the house (Scotus College) and adjacent buildings . . . and also grants temporary right to care the parishioners from the Missions that belong to the Parish. . . . . The Missions will be trusted temporary to the Province for their care and could be erected future Parishes and could be also offered to the Province.

When the Franciscan priests, brothers, and seminarians that belonged to the Saints Francis and James Province began to arrive in Hebbronville from Mexico, they were able to attend to the spiritual needs of a large number of missions in the surrounding communities. The following missions were under the care of the Franciscans: on the eastern side (Duval County) were Crestonio, Realitos, Concepcion, Rios, Ramirez, Tienditas, Copita, Santo Niño, Sejita, El Cibolo, La Salada, and Mazatlan; the southern side (Jim Hogg County) had Randado, Guerra, La Gloria, and Agua Nueva; and on the western side (Webb County) were Bruni, Torrecillas, Oilton, Laureles, San Pablo, Los Ojuelos, Mirando City, Aguilares, and Pescadito.

Today, the only missions that are in the care of the Franciscans are Sacred Heart Mission in Bruni, St. Bridget Mission in Oilton, and St. Agnes Mission in Mirando City, all located in Webb County.

As Hebbronville grew, people established neighborhoods on the south of the railroad. People living there found it difficult to walk from there to Our Lady of Guadalupe Church, especially in inclement weather. This was the primary reason it was decided to build a new chapel for Sunday Masses. The chapel was dedicated to the Immaculate Conception of the Blessed Virgin Mary and it came to be known as "Inmaculada," pictured left in 1953. The chapel included a small hall for catechism classes, social gatherings, and fundraising events.

The Inmaculada chapel was built on land donated by Angelita Ramírez. She gave three lots, located at the intersection of Draper Street and South Maria Avenue for the building. The lots measured 50 feet by 100 feet. The construction started in 1941 with the support of benefactors Juan M. García, Sinecio Gutiérrez, Fernando Ramírez, Jesús Peña, Manuel Barraz, Benito Garza, Zoila López, Lidia Garza, Aurora Barraz, Estela Ramírez, and Anita Molina, among others. It was approved by Fr. Hilario Núñez, pastor, and Fr. Fernando Cisneros, parochial vicar. Cinder blocks brought from Laredo and covered with stucco were used. Its floor was wood, and the ceiling had a decorative laminated cover donated by Peter Leyendecker from Laredo. Franciscan students from the Scotus College helped in the construction. On December 8, 1942, the chapel and the image of the Immaculate Conception, which, to this day, remains on the altar were blessed by Father Cisneros.

St. Bridget Mission Oilton, Texas, Webb County. The actual town of Oilton, founded in 1891, originally was located on the south side of the railroad and was named "Torrecillas" (little towers). In 1923, people living in Torrecillas moved to the north side of the railroad tracks and named their new location, Oilton, because oil had been discovered close by. The original chapel built in 1892 was also moved, pulled by mules, to its new location, thus making it the oldest of the Franciscan missions in this area. In the beginning, the mission was visited by priests from Aguilares, Texas. However, in 1926, the Franciscans from Hebbronville became responsible. In 1938, the sacristy was added. A brick exterior was applied to the church in 1977. St. Bridget Mission still belongs to Our Lady of Guadalupe Parish, and it is still administered by the Franciscans.

This is the St. Agnes Mission in Mirando City, Texas, Webb County. The townsite of Mirando City is on land granted to Nicolás Mirando. Originally it was a small ranching community. In April 1921, Oliver Winfield Killam brought in the first commercial oil well in the area. Quickly, he began to purchase land in Mirando Valley, and by September 1921, he started laying out the town of Mirando City. In December, a gusher at another drilling site ushered in an oil boom. Lots began selling rapidly, and the town quickly became a hub of activity. In that same year, the first chapel, made of wood, was built. In 1971, realizing the old church was badly deteriorated, the community and the Franciscans, represented by Fr. Alberto Hernandez, decided to build a new church made of brick and cement. The new church was dedicated to St. Agnes and blessed in 1972. The Franciscans continue to serve St. Agnes Mission.

This is the Sacred Heart Mission in Bruni, Texas, Webb County. The town was named after Antonio Bruni, an Italian immigrant who arrived in the area around 1877 and owned a general store and a ranch. Bruni became a station stop-over on the Texas-Mexican Railway about 1881, and by 1939, the population had increased with the discovery of the South Bruni oilfield. The first chapel was built in 1916 on land donated by the Bruni family. When the Franciscans arrived in Hebbronville in 1926, they took responsibility for the mission and started to build a new chapel made of wood—and dedicated it to the Sacred Heart of Jesus. That same year, Bishop Ledvina blessed the chapel and celebrated the Sacrament of Confirmation. In 1973, the sacristy was added, and in 1982, a brick exterior was added. It continues to be part of the Parish in Hebbronville, and it is still under the care of the Franciscans.

This is the St. Agnes Mission Hall in Mirando City. It was built in the 1920s and was used for catechism classes and community gatherings. During the construction of the new church, it was used for fundraising events. In 2005, it was replaced by a new hall.

When Sacred Heart Mission in Bruni was established, this hall was also built. This small room was also used for catechism classes and the mission's community gatherings. In 1987, a new building was constructed, replacing it, and in 2005, another hall was added to the Sacred Heart building complex.

Pictured is the Sacred Heart Mission in Realitos, Texas, Duval County. The community of Realitos was established on the Santos García Spanish land grant. In 1885, Realitos was described as "a settlement, also a ranch." Franco Cadena donated a lot to Msgr. Pedro Verdaguer, bishop of Corpus Christi, in 1888 to build a chapel. Pictured above is the first chapel made of wood dedicated to Our Lady of Guadalupe, in 1940. A priest from San Diego, Texas, would come by train once a week to celebrate Mass. The picture below is of the inside of the mission.

When the Franciscans arrived in Hebbronville, they took charge of the Realitos mission. In 1938, the Franciscans built the new chapel and dedicated it to the Sacred Heart of Jesus, pictured above. In 2000, when the Diocese of Laredo was created, the mission stayed in the Diocese of Corpus Christi under the care of the Benavides, Texas, parish. Below is a picture of the mission in Tienditas, Duval County, Texas, in 1936. The small township of Tienditas used to have a small chapel. Here, the Franciscans celebrated Mass every week. The community and the old chapel no longer exist.

This is the St. Peter Mission in Aguilares, Texas, Webb County. The community was named for brothers José, Locario, Francisco, Próspero, and Librado Aguilar, who established ranches in the area in the 1870s. Pictured above is the wooden chapel built in 1881. In 1892, Fr. Emilio J. Ylla was living in Aguilares and was in charge of the mission. By 1900, Fr. Miguel Puig was responsible for the chapel. The last priest to take charge was Fr. A. Serna, who began his service in 1902. When the Franciscan friars took charge of the parish in Hebbronville, St. Peter Mission became a Franciscan mission until the early 1960s when the people of the community slowly began to leave Aguilares, and it eventually died out. The picture below is of the residence of the priests.

St. Francis Mission Rios, Duval County, Texas. The community of Rios was founded by Dionisio Elizondo in 1835. The church was built in the early 1900s. Priests from San Diego would go every week to celebrate the sacraments. When the Franciscans arrived in 1926, Bishop Ledvina gave them this mission. In 1937, the chapel burned and the Franciscans used the school, pictured above, to celebrate Mass. In 1967, Bishop Gracida gave this mission to the care of the Premont Texas Parish. Pictured below is the mission in Sejita, Duval County, Texas, near Ramirez. The community and the chapel no longer exist.

This is the Immaculate Conception Mission in Concepcion, Texas, Duval County. Concepcion, locally called "La Chona," was named for Santa Cruz de Concepción, a land grant from the Spanish government to Francisco Cordente. The first church was built in 1879 by Fr. Claude Jaillet from the San Diego Parish. When the Franciscans arrived in 1926, Bishop Ledvina gave this mission to their care. In 1947, the Franciscans started to build a new church and modeled it after the Inmaculada chapel in Hebbronville. In 1967, the mission became part of the Premont Parish. Below is the Santo Niño de Atocha Mission in Duval County. Though the chapel no longer exists, in its time it was also under the care of the Franciscans.

This is the Our Lady of Guadalupe Mission in Ramirez, Texas, Duval County. Franciscans celebrated weekly Mass here. In 2000, it became part of the Premont Parish. The old chapel was demolished, and a new church was built. Below is Saint Raphael Chapel in Randado Ranch, Jim Hogg County. It is a private chapel built by the ranch owners in the 1850s and dedicated to the archangel Raphael. The first priests to celebrate Mass here were the Oblates from the valley. Although Franciscans do not administer the chapel, it is under the territory of the Hebbronville Parish.

After the Franciscans arrived in Hebbronville in 1926, Fr. Antonio Maria Gómez assigned Fr. Antonio Rábago to find another place in the Diocese of Corpus Christi for the formation of the new candidates to the Franciscan Order. Fr. Rábago met with Bishop Ledvina on August 24. Bishop Ledvina called John G. Kenedy, a patron of the Catholic Church and owner of La Parra Ranch, and asked him for help to find a place for the Franciscan postulancy. Kenedy offered his house in Sarita, Texas. It was the two-story, five-room, wooden house pictured here. Father Rábago returned to Mexico, but on September 13, 1926, Father Gómez who had initiated the project went to Sarita and took charge of the postulancy. Father Gómez made some improvements and adaptations to the house. On September 29, 1926, the first 27 postulant students and 5 Franciscan teachers arrived in Sarita. The Franciscans were in Sarita until 1930, when they moved the postulancy to Mexico.

Seven

FRANCISCAN LEGACY IN HEBBRONVILLE

Throughout almost a hundred years of Franciscan presence in Hebbronville, the community, that kindly received the friars looking for shelter, has been blessed. Since 1926, the Franciscan friars, with sacrificial efforts and service, have been dedicated to supporting the cultural, educational, and spiritual needs of Hebbronville and the surrounding communities that were and are located in Jim Hogg, Webb, and Duval Counties.

Soon after their arrival, the Franciscans started the spiritual care of the Catholic community that, with years, has grown, the building of a new church and its unique wooden altar handcrafted in Mexico, as well as all the liturgical furnishing and goods, are proof of the artistic and architectural legacy of the Franciscans. The Little Flower parochial school is a living testimony that the Franciscans were preoccupied with the education of children and future generations, in almost fifty years of service the school housed many generations of students. Today, the Franciscans lease their property for a daycare that assists the low-income community. The main local cemetery was founded by the Franciscans in 1932 and still operates.

Along with the beautiful church, the Franciscans built a seminary for the formation of future priests: the Scotus College, which is the preeminent architectural landmark in Hebbronville. Painted white and sitting on a large palm-lined green lawn, the Scotus College's segmental arched linear ambulatory crowning the ridge of its red Spanish-tiled roof, is visible for miles beyond the city limits. It is considered a treasure and a one-of-a-kind in the entire state of Texas. More than 250 men were educated in Hebbronville for the priesthood, some of whom would later become bishops. Today, it is used to provide religious instruction, host community events as a Parish Hall, and provide office space; for the establishment of the Franciscan Museum of Hebbronville; and as residence for the Franciscan friars.

Because of the scarcity of public schools, members of the Mexican community in Hebbronville—Asencio Martinez, Tomas Barrera, Dionisio and Severo Peña, and Francisco Barrera and Jose Angel Garza—opened their own *escuelita* (Spanish-language community school) and named it El Colegio Altamirano. The school was named in honor of Ignacio Manuel Altamirano, a novelist, poet, and journalist of Aztec heritage who also served as a Supreme Court justice in Mexico. El Colegio enrolled students from kindergarten to sixth grade and imported its material and textbooks from Mexico. The first teacher was Rosendo Barrera, who taught until 1907, when he died, and then sisters Adelina and Ernestina Carmona continued teaching. Pictured above are Adelina (first row, far left) and Ernestina (first row, far right) with students in 1908. The most remembered teacher is Emilia Dávila, who taught for over 30 years. She is pictured below with students in 1910.

Emilia Dávila was born in Saltillo, Coahuila, and was a graduate of the Normal School (teacher's college) in Saltillo. In her role as the sole teacher for decades and her pedagogical experience, she became the "intellectual mother" of Hebbronville's children. Above, she is pictured with the class of 1911, and below, she is with the class of 1915. In 1929, some women of the community with the support of the Franciscans, founded the Sociedad Josefa Ortiz de Dominguez to financially support the Colegio. After serving the community for more than 60 years, the Colegio Altamirano closed its doors in 1958. The building stands across the Scotus College. In 2019, the Sociedad donated the property to the Franciscan friars, who currently lease it to the Head Start Program, a federal program that provides comprehensive child development services to the community.

When the Franciscans arrived in Hebbronville in 1926, they realized there was a need for the educational and religious formation of Hebbronville's Catholic youth. With this in mind, Fr. Madueño, who was the pastor, initiated the idea to build a parochial school run by religious sisters. In 1927, a lot was donated by Viggo Kohler for a building. Fr. Madueño presented the project to Bishop Ledvina who approved it and made the first donation of $7,000 to start the construction. The Franciscans contracted Justo Alvarez, father of architect Jose Alvarez who designed and helped in the construction of the Scotus College and the new church. The construction began on July 21, 1930, and by September 26, it was completed, here pictured. It was blessed by Msgr. John Dobourgel under the patronage of St. Therese of Lisieux, thus the name of Little Flower School, fondly remembered as "El Convento" (the Convent) because the nuns who taught there also made it their residence.

On August 15, 1930, the religious sisters of the Siervas del Sagrado Corazon y de los Pobres arrived in Hebbronville from Mexico to teach in the new parochial school. Among the first sisters were María Eugenia, Inés de Jesús, and Celina de Jesús Silva. Since the facility was not completed until September, and the nuns were to teach and live in the building, they had to live temporarily in the Garza house and teach in the parish hall. Classes officially started on September 8, 1930. On October 31, the sisters moved into the Little Flower School. By the end of 1931, the school was completely equipped. Pictured here is one of the first generations of students.

This is a picture of the Little Flower School in 1961. The original building measured 84 feet by 30 feet and had three stories, a basement, and a small chapel that measured 8 feet by 14 feet. It had three doors: north, east, and the visitor's door to the south. The exterior of the building was of concrete. The floors on all levels were wood.

The fruits of the pedagogical and catechetical efforts that the sisters and friars brought to the parochial school have contributed to the cultural and spiritual formation of many generations that still cherish the memories of the *convento*. Some recall being sent to the dreaded *cubacha* when they misbehaved. Pictured here is a gathering with parents and students in 1952.

By 1940, the school had 95 students. In 1954, it was clear the school needed to be extended. Thanks to the generosity of Sarita Kenedy, a patron of the Catholic Church, a second building, the Sarita Kennedy East Hall, was added. This picture shows the East Hall. By 1955, the school had 265 students and also a middle school program.

In 1967, the Hermanas Misioneras de la Purísima Virgen María took charge of the school until 1969 when it was closed by Fr. José Gloria. This is a picture of one of the last groups. Over time, the building began to deteriorate. After several attempts to rehabilitate and restore it, the property was abandoned and condemned by Fr. Evencio Herrera in 2018.

The Franciscans were devoted to the cultural and spiritual development of Hebbronville's youth and, they also were diligent in their spiritual formation. Since their arrival and with the help of volunteer catechists, they prepared the children to receive sacraments. This is a picture of a Franciscan priest with children outside the first Scotus College building in 1938.

This is a unique photograph of the First Holy Communions celebrated by the Franciscans in Hebbronville. On November 7, 1926, after receiving classes from Father Ruiz, about 25 children celebrated their First Holy Communion. This picture was taken outside the parish office with the children who received their First Holy Communion along with their sponsors. In the back is Father Madueño, who celebrated the Mass.

Not only catechists taught children, but also the Franciscans did so too; even the seminarians used to help in their spiritual formation. Today, people still remember their lessons. This picture of Father Muñoz with a child outside the Realitos mission was taken in 1946.

One of the many traditions that Franciscans left in Hebbronville is the prayer of the Holy Rosary and the offering of flowers to the Blessed Virgin Mary by the children during the month of May. At the end of the month, a child was selected to crown the image of the Immaculate Conception. Pictured here is Isidro Gutierrez Jr., who had the honor to crown the Blessed Virgin.

Franciscans were also diligent in the spiritual formation of the parish groups and associations that worked together with them. This is a picture of some members of the Catholic Daughters along with Fr. Gonzalo Guzmán and other priests in a gathering held at the Little Flower School in 1962.

Men were also active in the Parish associations. Pictured here are members of the Sociedad Mutualista and Knights of Columbus in 1940. From left to right are (first row) José Alvarez, Pedro Nava, Juan B. Garza, Adolfo Vela, and Abelardo González; (second row) Sandalio Ramírez, Fr. Pedro Otálora, Fr. Agustín Ramírez, and Rafael García.

In addition to the cultural and spiritual legacy of the Franciscans, they also worked unceasingly in the construction, repairs, and restoration of Franciscan structures. Two main churches in Hebbronville, the majestic Scotus College compound buildings, the Little Flower School and its annex, and all the missions in the surrounding communities are the visible vestiges of the Franciscan legacy. In the picture above, Jose Alvarez and some workers stand in the new church bell tower during its construction. Below are some ladies of the Altar Society visiting the construction of one of the missions.

Other precious elements of the Franciscan legacy passed onto the community of Hebbronville are the Catholic traditions and the artistic and sacred furnishings, vessels, and vestments used for the liturgical celebrations. Franciscans have always been devoted to reverend with dignity and respect the sacred liturgy as part of their spirituality. In the picture to the left are the festivities celebrated in honor of the patron saint in the St. Peter mission in Aguilares. Below is a beautiful picture of the altar in the Sacred Heart Mission in Realitos, with the adoration of the Blessed Sacrament.

The main local cemetery, the Our Lady of Guadalupe New Hebbronville Cemetery, is administered by the Franciscans. On November 4, 1932, William W. Jones donated the lots. A few days later, on November 30, Br. Serafín Figueroa, one of the students of the Scotus College who was about to become ordained as a priest, died of bone consumption. This is the picture of his funeral.

The Sociedad Católica Mutualista raised funds to buy the first hearse for the use of the community. This is a picture of the blessing of the new hearse on April 3, 1938, held by (at right, from left to right) Father Zulaica, along with Mutualistas Adolfo Vela and Pedro Nava.

Since the arrival of the Franciscans in Hebbronville, their presence has marked and impacted the community. The Franciscan friars are an important part of the community. The residents appreciate their presence at the most important local events. People have worked together with Franciscans for the educational, cultural, and spiritual development of the community. These are pictorial proofs of the friendship between the people of Hebbronville and the Franciscans. Above, from left to right, are Fr. Pedro Otálora, Abelardo Gonzalez, and Jose Alvarez. Below is Br. Miguel Soria (second from left) and Fr. Bernardino Mora (fourth from left) with Rafael Garcia (center) and family.

Since their arrival, Franciscans have been devoted to the spiritual care of the Catholic community of Hebbronville. The building of a new church and its unique wooden altar handcrafted in Mexico, as well as all the liturgical furnishing and goods, are proof of the artistic gifts of the Franciscans to the community. Along with the beautiful church, the Franciscans also built an architecturally significant building, the Scotus College, which is recognized as a unique landmark in the entire region. These and all the buildings that still remain are the living testimony of the artistic and architectural legacy of the Franciscans.

The Franciscan friars have remained in Hebbronville for almost a hundred years. Their presence has influenced the educational and cultural development of the community as well as the spiritual formation and guidance of Catholic families of Hebbronville and its surrounding communities. With patience, sacrifice, and effort, the Franciscans have gifted the community with the spirit of their order. The people of Hebbronville are blessed for the presence of many friars over the years who gave up their lives in service to the people. In the same manner, Franciscans of the Jalisco Province are grateful and appreciative to this community, who received them with open arms and helped them survive. This is a picture of one of the last groups of Franciscan seminarians in Hebbronville.

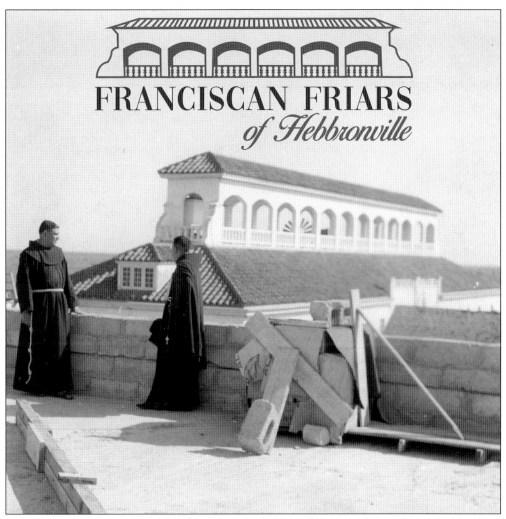

FRANCISCAN FRIARS
of Hebbronville

The Franciscan friars of Hebbronville are working diligently to revitalize and restore the Scotus College historic building. This architectural treasure of South Texas is a multipurpose facility: accommodating the Franciscan Museum of Hebbronville; the church office and classroom spaces; the Parish Hall for community events; and, lastly, serving as the residence of the Franciscan friars. Since 1926, the Franciscan friars of Hebbronville remain passionately committed to their mission of supporting and enhancing the cultural, educational, and spiritual needs of the people of Hebbronville and those in surrounding communities in Jim Hogg, Webb, and Duval Counties. Please help us continue our mission, feel free to visit us anytime, call, or send us an email if you need more information:

Franciscan Friars of Hebbronville
504 E. Santa Clara Street
Hebbronville, Texas 78361
Phone: (361) 527-3865
Email: FFHebbronville@gmail.com
Website: FFHebbronville.com

DISCOVER THOUSANDS OF LOCAL HISTORY BOOKS
FEATURING MILLIONS OF VINTAGE IMAGES

Arcadia Publishing, the leading local history publisher in the United States, is committed to making history accessible and meaningful through publishing books that celebrate and preserve the heritage of America's people and places.

Find more books like this at
www.arcadiapublishing.com

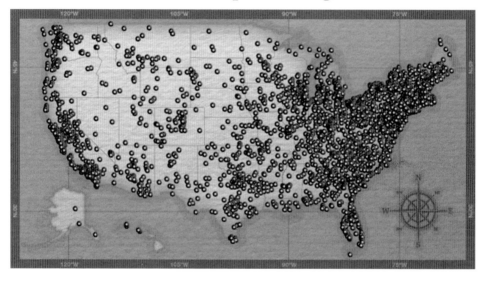

Search for your hometown history, your old stomping grounds, and even your favorite sports team.